THE RAP ON GANGSTA RAP

THE RAP ON GANGSTA RAP

WHO RUN IT?:
GANGSTA RAP AND
VISIONS OF BLACK VIOLENCE

BAKARI KITWANA

Third World Press • Chicago, IL

Published by:
Third World Press
P.O. Box 19730
Chicago, IL 60619

ISBN: 0-88378-175-1
Library of Congress Number: 94-90201

Front cover art by P.O.S.E. II

Back cover art by FX Crew:
            P.O.S.E. II, King B, and Per 1

Cover design by Denise O. Paultre

Manufactured in the United States
94 95 96 97 98 99   6 5 4 3 2 1

ACKNOWLEDGEMENTS

This work would not exist without the assistance, encouragement, and example of the Dance family, Haki R. Madhubuti, Sonia Sanchez, Joyce A. Joyce, JMJ, Denise O. Paultre, Acklyn Lynch, Pearl Cleage, Lynn Wade-Rochon, David Kelly, Kimberly Watkins, Jeffrey Montgomery, Mary Pattillo, Hashim Shomari, Tracy Sharpley, Michael Coburn, Dorian Sylvain, Jesse Carter, Monique Fortenberry, Rick Kittles, Judy Scully, Lasana Imani, Scot Brown, Lillian Rosa, Ron Rochon, Lee Copeland, Tone B. Nimble, and Kamau Tyehimba. Much respect, thanks, and appreciation.

CONTENTS

Preface

The Rap on Gangsta Rap intends to function as a handbook on the commercialization of rap music. The controversial association of gangsta rap with the escalating crisis of teen violence has initiated extensive public debate. It is a debate that can be heard in our homes and schools, in barbershops, beauty shops, and coffeeshops, at work, alongside basketball courts, on our playgrounds and in Congress. This discussion is often intense, and it never fails to generate a colorful range of emotions and opinions. However, much of what has been said, written, and continuously discussed opens a larger void than it fills. *The Rap on Gangsta Rap* addresses the larger questions of rap music and violence as it attempts to heal the growing rift between Black women and men as well as Black youth and adults.

The Rap on Gangsta Rap intends to promote more careful, critical thinking on the part of rap artists, rap enthusiasts, and the general public. It provides definitions for difficult, often unapproached, misunderstood, and misrepresented concepts, such as *hip hop culture* and *hardcore*, among others. It attempts to place the discussion of gangsta rap into the larger concerns of Black culture, Black struggle, women's struggle, the great disparity between America's minority economic elite and majority poor, and the extensive impact of white supremacy (racism) on Black world development. Most importantly, this work pushes against the barriers that obstruct meaningful dialogue.

The Rap on Gangsta Rap is about clarity: the development of rap music and its commercialization, the role of gun violence in marketing and advertising, the effects of the casual use of the words *nigger*, *bitch*, *hoe*, and others, the perceived generation gap, and the continuing need for Black enlightened empowerment.[1]

Its about rap. Signifying. The dozens. Black Culture. Music. Language. Definitions. Blacks. Race. Gender. Black art. Sexuality. Community. Consciousness. Creativity. Youth. Adults. Elders. Ancestors. Words. Politics. Economics. Media. History. Spirituality. Healing. Liberation. Life. And rap.

Bakari Kitwana
May 1994

THE RAP ON GANGSTA RAP

Black people are viewed as pitiful pawns in an international game of control and manipulation, and our worldwide misuse is an accepted by-product of business as usual.

Haki Madhubuti,
Black Men: Obsolete, Single, Dangerous?

When you're talking consciousness, nobody wants to listen....But if I was talking sex and all that nonsense, I'd get all the covers.

KRS-ONE,
Questions and Answers

Would you let the system get inside your head?...Would you let the system get inside your element?...Would you let the system make you kill your brotherman?...

Bob Marley,
Coming in From the Cold

Who Run it?:
Gangsta Rap and
Visions of Black Violence

The sophistication with which mass media chooses its issues, advances, retreats and moves on to the next without serious opposition to its contradictions and inconsistencies is one of the critical components that ensures white economic elite rule. Carefully noting the various approaches to such diverse issues as the Gulf War, David Koresh's Branch Davidians and the War in Bosnia-Herzegovina to the Nation of Islam/Anti-Defamation League clash, the Clarence Thomas/Anita Hill affair, and the alleged shooting incidents involving rap artists can be a crash course in American politics, racism, sexism, and corporate elitism—all at the same time. While the issues seem to change daily, as public sentiment and discussion are artfully manipulated, the status quo remains unchallenged. Since the media heightened its ongoing Black attack with a recent focus on so-called gangsta rap music,[2] various simple-minded generalizations about Black people and rap music have gained popularity amongst a broad range of "respected" public officials, academicians, and journalists who serve as springboards for influencing public policy and opinion.

EXPERTS AND MASS CONFUSION

In a recent *New York Times* op-ed article,[3] Brown University's American Studies professor Michael Dyson offered one of the most saddening defenses of rap music presented to date: Professor Dyson insisted that rap music is not responsible for sexism and misogyny in the Black community. Rather, he suggests, the Black church, despite its Eurocentric Christian legacy, is the source of these tendencies:

> If blacks really want to strike at the heart of sexism and misogyny in our communities, shouldn't we take a closer look at one crucial source of these blights....the black church...has also given us an embarrassing legacy of sexism and misogyny.

And who can ever forget the now historic 1990 censorship trial of 2 Live Crew's Luther Campbell, in which Harvard's W.E.B. DuBois Scholar Henry Louis Gates, Jr. testified that lewd sexual violence was not advocated in Campbell's concert performance of selections from his album, *As Nasty as They Wanna Be?* Gates insisted that Campbell, as an artist and wordsmith, is merely "signifying."

> There is no call to violence here. What you hear is humor, great joy and boisterousness. It's a joke. It's parody, and parody is one of the most venerated forms of art.[4]

Dyson's perspective parrots the economic elite party line in blaming the victim, but Gates' rationalization breaks new ground. He infers that the use of sexist and misogynist language as a joke is a phenomenon of Black culture. Such belittling critiques of Black people from Black scholars, under the auspices of defending rap music, is just the tip of the iceberg.

In February 1994, Representative Cardiss Collins (D-IL) and Senator Carol Mosley-Braun (D-IL) initiated Congressional hearings on so-called gangsta rap and the effects of "violent and demeaning music lyrics on our nation's youth." This critical questioning is important and necessary. Yet if these inquiries do not explore the economic elite's violent and demeaning practices and values as well as their extensive influence throughout America's institutions, these efforts will not escape the confines of mainstream society's ongoing anti-Black attack.

Amidst the public's increasing concern about the escalation of teen gun violence, rap music is often viewed as a major contributor to the problem. Most often, these critiques of rap are one-dimensional: they excuse the society and make broad-sweeping generalizations about rap music and Black youth as violent, criminal-prone, anti-social, and certainly rebellious. These types of accusations are typical in a society where the public is programmed (from education and politics to mass media) to seek quick-fix, easy answers. It is much less threatening to the status quo (as well as jobs, positions, and conditional friendships) to place the blame on Blacks. Yet, exactly how does the economic elite's influence on the commercialization of rap music converge with Black art, Black creativity, Black rage, America's ever-increasing technology, and the ruling economic elite's role in creating public images of Black people? Indeed, there are elements of rap music that alienate Black youth from one another, glorify violence, rebel on various levels, and further complicate mass media representations and definitions of Black men and women. But this is just one side. Some aspects of rap music demonstrate the distinctiveness and resilience of Black culture and insist that rap music is a valid musical art form that cannot be simply dismissed or narrowly defined.

RAP AND THE BLACK MUSICAL TRADITION

From its emergence in the South Bronx as early as 1974, rap music as an expression of various aspects of Black life was not new. Yes,

there are elements of rap music that are techno-
logically specific to the late-1900s, but Black
America has always been innovative in originat-
ing new musical art forms that reflect social
reality. Various elements central to Black musical expression remain unchanged, from Negro
spirituals, blues, gospel, jazz, and be-bop to R&B,
and rap: creative word-usage, call and response,
signifying, and rhythmic poetics (the cultural
specifics). As part of this continuum, rap music
gains validity. Anyone who suggests that rap
music is outside of this tradition is displaying
his/her unfamiliarity with Black culture.

Blacks have always rapped to music, as
we find word play in all of our musical artforms.
"Godfather of Soul" James Brown, Sarah Vaughn,
Aretha Franklin, Sweet Honey in the Rock's
Bernice Reagon, Pharoah Sanders and others all
beat a rhythm out of words. There is rhythm and
rhyme in the poetry of Countee Cullen, Claude
McKay, Sterling Brown, Amiri Baraka, Sonia
Sanchez, Gwendolyn Brooks, Mari Evans and
countless others. The 1960s Black Fire poets
"rapped" extensively. In recording *Medasi* and
Rise Vision Comin with the Washington, DC based
Nationhouse Positive Action Center, Haki
Madhubuti linked his poetic insight to an avant
garde jazz beat. The 1970s arrived with the

rhythmic words and drum beat of The Last Poets and bluesologist Gil Scott-Heron's politically-charged, carefully rhymed melodies.

The distinctiveness and relevance of Black English was thoroughly documented by Geneva Smitherman (*Talkin' and Testifyin': the Language of Black America* and *Black Talk: Words, and Phrases from the Hood to the Amen Corner*), Lorenzo Turner (*Africanisms in the Gullah Dialect*), J.L. Dillard (*Black English*) and others. H. Rap Brown in his *Die Nigger Die* recalls the influence of Blacks' use of language, via the dozens and signifying, on his personal development—informing us that his name, like most, was given because it signified his special gifts and his identity. The point is that rap as Black musical and oral expression is not wholly new.

Because music is a part of our day-to-day reality, as that reality evolves so must the music. We should welcome rap music because it demonstrates our ability to move beyond stagnation. This breath of fresh air was particularly rejuvenating in the late 1970s and early 1980s as African Americans continued to redefine our existence beyond the illusions of the integration/accommodation age of Black elected officials.

Critical to the development of rap music as an artform was the sampling, mixing, cutting, and scratching "D.J.," whose role evolved from the Jamaican concept of toasting.[5] The emergence of rapping in fast or slow rhythmic, spoken, repetitive words over the instrumental beat of a popular R&B (or funk) song or drum- and bass-heavy synthesized beats followed several years later. At its origin, rap music could be more easily defined. Rap artist KRS-ONE refers to this as "the original way."[6] The contributions of rap music pioneers Cool D.J. Herc, Africa Bambaata, Love Bug Starski, Grandmaster Caz, Busy B, Melle Mel, Cowboy, Scorpio, and others are instructive here. This original hardcore rap was invigorated by the critical influence of basement, house and block parties (tapping into street lights as power sources), the beat-box, D.J. battles, etc. The importance of sampling the grassroots, soulful sound of James Brown, "Godfather of Funk" George Clinton, and others cannot be overlooked. Additionally, rap music's New York City beginning is important; the urban roots of rap explain much about its nuances. Finally, the economic reality for Blacks during the late 1970s and early 1980s certainly impacted raps emergence. None of these influences can be forgotten in discussing rap's origins.

Despite this self-styled, "independent," and grassroots development at its origins, the influence of corporate elite commercialization[7] on rap music must be considered in order to understand the various images of rap music and hip hop culture that are with us today. Rap music has been altered significantly and, more often than not, contaminated by this process of commercialization. This phenomenon is not specific to rap music, but is often the case when cultures and people are commodified. Rap music's increasing visibility in addition to the increasing influence exerted onto rap by outside forces (*i.e.,* corporate elite, academicians, politicians, and mass media) has found these original definitions redefined, most often in the best interest of the ruling economic elite. Any critique of rap music and/or hip hop culture that does not consider this factor is either purposefully deceptive or terribly naive.

HIP HOP CULTURE, POPULAR CULTURE, AND BLACK CULTURE

For the sake of clarity (due to the extensive dissemination of misinformation about rap music), analyses of rap music must distinguish between rap music and hip hop culture; popular culture and Black culture; and hip hop culture and Black culture. The terms "rap music" and "hip hop culture" are not synonymous, but they are used interchangeably by some "experts." Additionally, hip hop culture and Black culture are not identical. Graffiti art, breakdancing, rap music, style of dress, attitude, verbal language, body language, and urban-influenced lifestyles are all aspects of hip hop culture. In fact, throughout the early 1980s, breakdancing, and graffiti art were both widely influenced by New York youth with various ethnic backgrounds—including Puerto Rican American, Dominican American, and Caribbean American. Similarly, the technological impact and the New York City metropolitan, urban setting all suggest a cross cultural, not exclusively Black setting that laid the foundation for the emergence of hip hop culture.

Although some elements of hip hop culture are indeed expressions of Black culture, hip hop culture as a culture cannot be defined or discussed as a carbon copy of Black culture. Hip hop culture and Black culture are as distinctive entities as are American culture and Black American culture. Just as there are African retentions present in the African American experience, various aspects of Black American culture permeate and influence both hip hop culture and commercial popular culture.

The term "popular culture" is routinely distinguished as something less valuable or less useful than authentic culture. This essay does not intend to duplicate that distinction. Popular culture can be useful and is valuable. The question is useful to whom, valuable to whose best interest? There is nothing wrong with expressions of a culture being popularized, consumed in mass, or adapted across cultures. Yet, in a capitalist economy, when corporate industry commercializes aspects of Black culture, most often, there is little or no concern for the art or culture. The ultimate objective is profit and because of this lack of sensitivity, that culture becomes distorted. Most certainly, Black folks' participation in commercial popular culture does not mean that these distorted images of Blacks and Black culture are accurate representations of Black culture simply because the transmitter is Black. Neither does the process of commercialization of aspects of Black culture by definition extract their Blackness. However, the trend of corporate commercialization of various Black cultural expressions has been toward manipulation (1) in the form of stereotypical characterizations of Blacks or (2) in suggesting that popularization has transformed the Black cultural expression from Black culture into "universal," mainstream culture (*read*, European, white culture). Thus, if one makes the mistake of uncritically associating Black culture with commercial popular culture, one is likely to attribute ideas, values, and phenomena to Black culture that are distorted by-products and creations of corporate commercialization. Because aspects of Black culture have been affected by America's multi-cultural (though often Eurocentric) society, the depth to which these technological, urban, and sometimes oppressive influences infiltrate Black America and commercialized rap music cannot be simply ignored.

IMPACT OF COMMERCIALIZATION ON RAP'S EVOLUTION

One of the primary catalysts responsible for the popularization of rap music was the music video. Michael Jackson's 1983 movie-styled "Thriller" music video opened corporate industry's eyes to a virtually untapped goldmine: selling the Black musical concept to consumers directly into their own homes via the music video. In 1984, Run-DMC's "Rock Box" video broke this ground for rap music with heavy rotation on MTV.[8] Rap music easily went beyond the influence of R&B because of its cross cultural appeal to youth.

Without question, the music video heightened rap music's commercialization. Part of the result of this commercialization is evident in rap music videos on MTV (*Yo MTV Raps*), initiated in 1989 and followed by BET (*Rap City*), *The Box*, and the now defunct *Pump It Up* (Fox TV). Also critical were interviews of rap artists on *The Arsenio Hall Show* (Paramount Pictures) as well as rap coverage in *The Source*, *Vibe*, and other magazines often influenced by economic elite concerns. These television programs and magazines are heavy corporate advertising mediums. In terms of capitalist economics and corporate behavior, corporations rarely support efforts that do not advance their financial goals.[9] Certainly, such corporations are not interested in developing rap music as an artform or in defining and protecting Black community interest.

The effort to commercialize rap was accompanied from the beginning by the recording industry's attempt to "cross over" rap music in the same way that Michael Jackson, Lionel Richie, and other R&B artists had "succeeded" in "crossing over" to non-Black audiences. However, in the process of crossing over, artists often alienate themselves from the Black community. The commercial popular success of cross over rap music has been distinguished by its ability to maintain its Black audience *and* maintain acceptance as an authentic Black voice.

This commercialized vision of rap music carried with it various aspects (though not all) of hip hop culture, giving the entire country access to a phenomenon that is often seen as exotic. The response of many white suburban youth to this phenomenon—dressing in rebellious hip hop "fashion," listening to rap music, and adopting and often misunderstanding the language of Black youth—is not unprecedented. (Recall blues, jazz, and du-wop.) The impact of this white gaze has been a tremendous surge in rap music record sales to white suburban youth.

In the November 1991 issue of the *New Republic*, David Samuels reports that based upon *Billboard*'s national sales totals, suburban white male teens are rap music's greatest buying audience.[10] This statement has been repeated as fact by many and rarely questioned in print. What Samuels does not reveal is the method by which *Billboard* compiles its data. *Billboard's* charts are based on the monthly findings of SoundScan, a computerized tracking system that logs over-the-counter sales. SoundScan currently tracks sales activity for 70 percent of the market. SoundScan insists that their estimated figures take into account the 30 percent of the market that is not on line. This tracking system does not include any demographic data. Thus, SoundScan relies on SoundData, a research group that conducts monthly survey panels of 1500 to 2000 active music consumers.

Based on both SoundScan and SoundData information, rap is purchased mainly by teenagers. SoundData's monthly surveys indicate that rap's greatest buying audience is white male suburban teens. According to SoundScan because "there are more whites in the U.S. than Blacks," and because SoundData's monthly surveys suggest overwhelming sales to white teens "it is a fair assumption to say white teens are rap's greatest buying audience."[11] However, because SoundScan does not log any demographic information and does not represent all record sales, and because SoundData surveys at best only 24,000 "active" music consumers annually, the claim that suburban white male teens are the greatest buying audience for rap music reflects an estimated guess only, not concrete numbers.

Assertions of this type indicate that corporate America remains locked into the assumption that Black and Latino youth are unpredictable consumers. Corporate industry seems more confident in the lucrative possibilities for the rap industry if white youth are predominantly represented as consumers. Understanding the historic white gaze, SoundScan and corporate recording studios use racist assumptions as confidence-building measures for advertisers and related interests. While media and corporate industry push the idea (race-baiting) that white teen listeners are fascinated with these images of Blackness, (Black youth as icons of rebellion and coolness, Black sexuality and street life as exotic) much of the gaze seems to be coming from corporate industry itself. Corporate America has preconceived notions of who Black youth are and a vision of who they should be and these images are represented in the style of rap it focuses on, gangsta rap and recreational rap (more about that later). Simultaneously, both types of rap music have proven marketable to white, Black, and Latino teens.

With the commodification of "Blackness" through rap music's commercialization, rap music entered the lip synch, synthesizer age. In this context, rap music is refined and packaged for sales' sake with two dominant trends. First, there is the attempt to emerge as a variation of R&B artists, focused on singing, dancing, and/or "profiling." The actual concept of rap becomes secondary. Lights, posturing, and hype become the focus rather than rap as an artform.[12] In effect, this is diluted rap music, saturated with current popular images of R&B (*i.e.* Salt-N-Pepa's "Whatta Man," MC Hammer's "You Can't Touch This"). Also packaged and sold is the so-called gangsta image (i.e. NWA, Onyx, Eazy E), the supposedly raw insider's look into Black urban street life via crime, sexuality, and sexual violence.

The commercialized, diluted rap image is straight-forward. On the other hand, the fact that the "gangsta" image is often accompanied by a hardcore lyrical style and sound complicates generalized attacks on "gangsta" rap. Hardcore rap music is not limited solely to "gangsta" rap and was not spawned by commercialization. The hardcore sound preserves much of the original essence of rap:

1) community-centered and responsive;
2) the music's sound is characterized by hard, potent beats, what is referred to as "boom-bap," originality in rap style (not attempting to imitate or duplicate another's rap style or lyrics), and creative manipulation of words (flow);
3) the rapper's voice becomes a rhythmic instrument, beating out a rhythm in words.

Hardcore rappers are not studio creations. For them, the ability to "free style" is honored, and lip synching is unacceptable. Rapper Doug E. Fresh adds a critical component to this definition and our understanding of hardcore in his description of what he calls "hip hop music":

> It has to be from the heart. It has to be something
> that you live. It can't be something that you
> just come out and do. It has to be *on the spiritual*
> *level where you just come out of your spirit* and
> say what you really feel.[13] (emphasis added)

The spiritual component is one that is rarely acknowledged in rap music, but is as present in hardcore rap music as it is in the most profound gospel, jazz, R&B, etc. It is not spiritual in terms of any specific religion. It reflects a sense of African spirituality and humanism: an understanding of the interconnected, the strangely balanced but dialectic nature of life.[14] For points of reference, listen to and study KRS-ONE's "The Original Way," "Like a Throttle," and "Higher Level," Ice Cube's "The Nigga Ya Love to Hate," MC Lyte's "Cappucino," A Tribe Called Quest's "Scenario," Doug E. Fresh's "The Show," Queen Latifah's "U.N.I.T.Y.," 2Pac's "Keep Your Head Up," Dana Dane's "Cindafella," Das EFX's "Mike Checka," EPMD's "Head Banger," and "Listen to My Demo," and Gang Starr's "Just to Get a Rep."

Although various small independent recording companies initiated the production, publishing, and marketing of rap records, larger record companies such as MCA Records, Warner Brothers Records, Capitol-EMI Music, Polygram

Records, Sony Music Entertainment Company (formerly CBS Records, Incorporated), and BMG Music soon realized the profit potential and during the late 1980s bought out or became distributors for several of these independent labels. This restructuring of the recording industry in regard to rap music effectively reinforced corporate control over distribution.

All of these large record companies are subsidiaries of multi-billion dollar international corporate conglomerates—several with annual sales in excess of 30 billion dollars. Only one of the parent companies, Time Warner, Incorporated (which owns Warner Records) is based in the United States. MCA Records is a subsidiary of Japan-based Matshushita Electrical Corporation, BMG Music is a subsidiary of Germany-based Bertelsmann Corporation, CBS records is owned by Japan-based Sony Music Entertainment, Incorporated, Polygram Records is a subsidiary of Netherlands-based Phillips Electronics, Incorporated, and Capitol EMI Records is a subsidiary of England-based Thorn EMI.[15]

These enormous corporate conglomerates are involved in the recording industry from top to bottom with operations in England, Germany, Japan, South Africa, Mexico, Brazil, Denmark, Italy, Argentina, Austria, Spain, France, Norway, and many other countries. Their business interests focus primarily on communications and entertainment—cable television, magazine and book publishing, movie theaters, identifying, developing and producing talent, manufacturing, producing and distributing film, records, compact discs, cassettes, videos, televisions, VCRs, camcorders, etc. They also branch out into areas as diverse as plastic card manufacturing, developing security systems, repairing military and civilian ships, manufacturing medical diagnostic imaging and radiotherapy equipment, and data systems, and imaging devices. They have ownership in such companies as Universal Studios, Book of the Month Club, Sports Illustrated, Rent-A-Center, Norelco, Magnavox, Columbia Pictures, Great America and Great Adventure Amusement Parks, Loews Theatres, HBO, Cablevision, Motown, Time Magazine, JVC, Panasonic and many others.[16]

Given the extensive influence of these international corporations, commercialized rap music dominates magazine, television (music videos), and radio. It is not simply that there is an audience for "gangsta" rap music. Corporate industry has realized a consumer desire and has nurtured a taste that it has extensively exploited and continues to exhaust. In the process, it has distorted aspects of Black culture and hip hop culture. Often highlighted are those aspects of rap which, despite their seemingly anti-establishment, angry, and street-life presentations, (1) do not threaten the status quo, (2) reinforce negative stereotypes about Blacks, (3) manipulate these stereotypes to increase sales, and (4) move rap music further away from its grassroots origins.

Despite the recent increase of rappers creating their own labels, larger corporations continue to control distribution channels. In most cases, this forces rap artists to come to terms with what is seen by corporate owned recording studios as currently marketable in order to secure any serious level of mass distribution. Because of the corporate structure's dominant voice in the rap music industry, most artists if they want to be deemed "successful" are forced to maintain a style and image which often compromises the rap artists' values or their attempt to elevate the artform.

Countless artists in search of securing record deals report that they are often told that their message is not hard enough, that they are too clean cut, that "hardcore" is what is selling now, or that the world has enough prophets.[17] Regardless of the exact phrase, essentially the message is that "gangsta" rap is "in" and to be successful as a rapper one must be aligned with the corporate industry's agenda. For example, MC Hammer's image has gone from a clean cut, dancing, almost religious rapper to a gangsta style almost overnight. Vanilla Ice has undergone a similar transformation. Once content is manipulated in this fashion, many artists must struggle with their own value system. This pull between their values and the "bottom line" forces many rappers to compromise their integrity.

Due to their extensive influence on the industry, corporate recording companies have ultimately established the boundaries for much of the discourse about rap music, even within the Black community. Too often rap artists' styles and lyrics and Black community reaction to them are the result of corporate visions. Certainly, the recording industry's current focus, with its distorted images of Blackness and its emphasis on "sales first" effectively undermines hip hop's potential as an agent for social change.[18]

EMANCIPATED "NIGGERS AND BITCHES" FOR SALE

Some commercialized rap achieves a hardcore sound and maintains *some* elements of "original" rap (developmental message, flow, innovative style and/or hard beats) that are progressive. Although a rap song can be hardcore, have a hardcore beat and vocal rap style, it can simultaneously be regressive in its lyrical content. This dynamic is central to the "does rap music promote violence?" debate. Much of this was fueled by the hardcore sound but regressive lyrics and tremendous sales of Niggaz With Attitude's *Niggaz 4 Life* (over 900,000 copies sold within the first week's release), Dr. Dre's *The Chronic* (over 3 million sold), and Snoop Doggy Dogg's *Doggy Style* (over one million sold in its first few months).

The impetus for these attacks outside of the Black community is often seasoned with racist overtones. Yet, there are many within our community that resist "gangsta" rap music because of its very negative and anti-Black implications. However, young listeners who appreciate the hardcore sound feel that rap as a whole is under attack. These rap enthusiasts view the attack on regressive lyrics as an attack on rap music and Black youth in general.

In defending rap, some insist that words such as *bytch, hoe*, and *nigga* do not have to be negative if one chooses not to view them as negative. When asked about the use these terms in a recent National Public Radio interview, Ice T responded, "That's how we are...that's how we talk in the ghetto...it's a Black thang."[19] Others, rap artists and rap enthusiasts argue that by frequently using these words, they can be reclaimed and redefined. (Notice the written and spoken reclamation insists n-i-g-g-a-z or n-i-g-g-a-s, never n-i-g-g-e-r-s; and b-y-t-c-h, not b-i-t-c-h, *i.e.*, 2 Pac's "Strictly for My Niggaz" and Snoop Doggy Dogg's "For all my Niggaz and Bytches"). Still, many insist that the rap lyrics are multi-layered (as in "you're my nigger and you ain't gonna get no bigger" as opposed to "no niggers allowed"). They argue that the historically negative words do not simply apply to stereotypical definitions, suggesting a hoe (whore) can be anyone who is getting pimped, such as rap artists by record companies, not solely women for sex.

Most who condone the use of the words in rap lyrics insist that when the rappers use these derogatory words in a negative context, such terms do not apply to themselves, all Blacks, or all women, but to some people ("I know *I* ain't no bitch, hoe, skeezer, or trick" is a general response often articulated). Such rationalizations never question the underlying logic of reclaiming as positive concepts that are negative in their intent and origin. Cultural critic Haki Madhubuti argues that such historic politically-charged words cannot be de-stereotyped:

> There are certain words...that are debilitating to us, no matter how often they are used. Such a word is nigger....A nigger, which is a pitiful and shameful invention of Europeans, cannot be de-stereotyped by using it in another context, even if the users are Black and supposedly politically correct (they are mostly young and unaware). A nigger is a nigger is a nigger and white folks love to hear us denigrate each other.... We can all visualize a 'Ghetto,' but can we conceive of a liberated community? Anyone can rap reality. Only artists have vision of a better world.[20]

The words "bitch," "whore," and "nigger" are terms applied to people to identify them as sub-human. What is problematic about the use of these terms by rap artists is the ease with which those artists participate in the commodification and distortion of "Blackness" and, therefore, their own degradation. In these contexts, Black women and men are objectified and these distorted images are bought and sold as music.

HARDCORE RAPS AND GENERATION GAPS

These diverse opinions that accompany this "rap attack" and the various defenses against it validate the myth of a generation gap in understanding and appreciating rap music. If indeed there is a gap, it is the void in our collective understanding of the continuum that Black culture necessitates. Too many Black youth lack an intimate understanding of Black culture, history, and struggle. This limits not only the music's possibilities as a source of Black empowerment, but its possibilities as a source of Black resistance to cultural assimilation via lack of control (from creation to distribution). Likewise, many Black adults fail to recognize the Black cultural qualities that persist in rap music. All of this is further complicated by the fact that the hardcore elements which exist in "gangsta" rap are often used by the economic elite influenced mass media to push, even in supposedly positive presentations on rap, anti-Black messages—suggesting that all hardcore rap music is regressive. This misinformation campaign has been so effective that today many uninformed listeners readily associate the term "hardcore" with "gangsta" rap, using the two terms interchangeably. Contrary to popular opinion, gangsta rap does not define hardcore rap music and this confusion is a gross misrepresentation.

Critiques of rap music cannot continue to ignore these distinct differences between hardcore rap music and commercially influenced rap music. Instead of jumping on the "bash hip-hop" bandwagon, critics of rap music (whether music critics, community activists, journalists or academicians), if they are to be taken seriously, must offer informed analyses that should include, at a minimum, listening to and studying the music.

Despite the continuing presence of hardcore rap artists, the commercialized vision of rap music—because of resources, power, and influence—dominates. The dominant (mainstream) presence of commercialized rap confused and continues to confuse many. In fact, some people's primary access to rap music and first contact with elements of hip hop culture—from teen listeners, budding rappers, and the general public to music critics and academicians—was via rap videos and tracks that received air play (on radio) as well as rap artists' newspaper, magazine, radio and television interviews and/or coverage. (The rap concert as it is known, is a relatively recent phenomenon, dating from the late 1980s.) In some instances, this has allowed for redefinition and expansion of the concept of rap music. Simultaneously, the motivation is profit, not necessarily good music, and the result is often imitation.

Another result of the dominance of commercialized rap is white rap artists (such as Vanilla

Ice, The Beastie Boys, House of Pain, and others) who don hip-hop dress style as a uniform, adopt Black urban youth body language, patterns of speech, vernacular word usage, assume (or pretend) that they understand Black culture as well as hip-hop culture, and attempt to "universalize" rap music. This appropriation of Black youth culture goes beyond national borders to the international level and similarly impacts jazz, blues, and R&B. This tendency is not limited to white rappers, but persists among performers who do not write their own lyrics and who co-opt a "street" stage persona.

Similarly, various academicians and journalists continue to co-opt Black urban youth culture under the guise of authority on Black culture and/or legitimate Black insider's voice. Yet, because of their failure to study hip hop culture and Black culture and listen to the music, as well as their social distance from the Black and hip hop communities, they only contribute to the misinformation by promoting false definitions and images of rap music and hip-hop culture.[21] Many of these critics suggest that all hardcore rap music contains, as one writer writes:

> graphic depictions of sexual conquests, drug use and gangs [imagery] and...glorification of violence towards women and homosexuals.[22]

These type of critiques repeatedly appear in newspaper and magazine articles that cover the ongoing discussion of "gangsta" rap's relationship to escalating teen violence. Because of their own misconceptions and faulty definitions, rarely do such critiques clarify the debates. Ultimately, they generate more unanswered questions than they resolve.

THE POLITICS OF RAP LYRICS

Despite the prominence of misleading critiques, rap music is not beyond criticism. In fact, careful examination and appreciation of rap music allows one to distinguish between aspects of rap music that are valuable and aspects of rap music that are destructive to the Black community and the general public. It is here that careful critiques of rap music gain the greatest validity and potential for positive impact. Professor of Black Studies Maulana Karenga categorizes rap music as follows: (1) player/lover, (2) gangster, (3) teacher, (4) fun lover, and (5) religious.[23] The value of categorization is that it more effectively isolates various tendencies and thus provides for the possibility of more carefully examination. Further, it allows critics to avoid inaccurate generalizations about rap music that are demeaning to Black people. For the purposes of this discussion, consider the following three categories: recreational rap, conscious rap, and sex-violence rap. These categories focus on lyrical content, not style (*i.e.* hardcore, "original way" vs. commercialized rap music). In some cases, the categories overlap. Some rap artists may even on the same album or song traverse all three.

Recreational Rap. Recreational rap encompasses both what Dr. Karenga defines as player/lover and fun lover. Rap lyrics that fall in this category tend to approach various themes central to R&B. Topics deal with sex and love, are sometimes non-sensical, and often engage in self-aggrandizement, boasting, bragging, signifying and the dozens. Examples of these recreational lyrics are The Fresh Prince's "Summertime," Salt-N-Pepa's "Push It" and "Shoop," and LL Cool J's "Around the Way Girl."

Conscious Rap.[24] Conscious Rap is characterized by lyrics whose content is either Black conscious and/or politically conscious. Political activists are quoted, paraphrased or sampled (Malcolm X, Kwame Toure, Louis Farrakhan, etc.). Socially conscious issues, such as sexual awareness, also define conscious rap. The emphasis is more on the collective rather than the individual. Signifying and the dozens are not to be ruled out. This category is compatible with Maulana Karenga's classification "teacher." Examples are Public Enemy's "Fight the Power," KRS-ONE's "Sound of the Police" and "Who Are the Pimps," The Coup's "Funk," EPMD's "Crossover," Poor Righteous Teachers' "Speaking Upon a Black Man" and "Each One Teach One," Brand Nubians' "Wake Up" and "Drop the Bomb" and from rap's early days, Grandmaster Flash and the Furious Five M-Cs' "The Message."

Sex-Violence Rap. The term Sex-Violence rap is derived from the title of KRS-ONE's album, *Sex and Violence*, where he critiques the dominance of commercialized rap music and rap's movement away from "the original way." What Dr. Karenga terms "gangster" fits this category. Sex-violence lyrics advance sexist language, encourage negative and regressive attitudes about women and homosexuals (often promoting violence against both), and aggrandizes the gun as a symbol of macho power, a cure-all for disputes (mostly petty) among Blacks and less often between Blacks and the cops. It is important to stress that the problem is not with artists exploring notions of erotica and/or sensuousness, but with graphic and often crude, violent, self-hating, women-hating, and anti-Black, abusive sexual representations. Just as in

33

the other categories, the dozens and signifying remain critical. Yet, when analyzing sex-violence rap lyrics, it is essential to distinguish between a rapper who is signifying with light parody, in the blues tradition,[25] and a rapper whose vulgar, profane, and insensitive lyrics advocate street culture.

Although it is necessary to make this distinction in category, it is equally important to indicate that this sex-violence culture permeates much of today's rap music, glorifying some of these concepts and/or subtly reinforcing aspects of this worldview. For example, Queen Latifah's "Just Another Day" and Akinyele's "I Love Her" would not be considered "gangsta" raps. Yet, their characterizations of urban life, Black-on-Black gun violence, Black male-female relationships, women-hating, sexual violence, or extreme individualism reinforce images of the sex-violence worldview commonly described as "gangsta" rap.

While sex-violence rap lyrics are sometimes politically informed and exhibit various levels of political consciousness (accurately describing the social reality of some oppressed situations), they use racism as an excuse for not moving beyond problem-recognition to enlightened action. The resulting rationale vacillates between violence

for violence sake and white racism / Black oppression as an excuse for violent nihilism (social
apathy, *i.e.*, the lyrics of MC Eiht's "Streiht up
Menace," the theme song for the film *Menace II
Society*, which portrayed Black male youth as
mindless, animalistic, gun-toting thugs).

Such lyrics and accompanying imagery via
mass media are popularly called "gangsta" rap,
but the term "gangsta" rap is misleading and has
become increasingly vague. The term sex-violence intends to be more specific and includes
lyrics that are compatible with the "gangsta" rap
worldview, but are not generally identified as
"gangsta" rap.

As Dr. Karenga emphasizes, such lyrics are
too often disrespectful of Black people and too
quick to reclaim and reinforce negative stereotypes about Blacks.[26] The repeated use of words
within these lyrics like *bytch*, *hoe*, and *nigga*,
articulates visions of Black inferiority as clearly
as those trumpeted by leading neo-conservative
white "thinkers." Some of this promotion of
negative street culture developed exclusive of
recording studios, but the recording industry's
participation in advancing this negative street
culture can neither be ignored nor dismissed.
Examples are NWA's "She Swallowed it," Snoop
Doggy Dog's "Gz up Hoes Down," Kool G Rap's

"Talk Like Sex," Dr. Dre's "Bitches Ain't Shit (but hoes and trix)," MC Eiht's "Caps Get Peeled," South Central Cartel's "Gang Stories," and Ice Cube's "Tales From the Westside."

COMMUNITY NEED AND COMMERCIAL DESIRE

What has been characterized for the past several years as a recession is clearly a larger global economic shift. The economic elite continues to accumulate wealth at the expense of the majority poor and is an increasingly smaller segment of the American and world populations, respectively. As the so-called underclass rapidly expands and the so-called middle-class continues to jockey to hold on to its preassigned, depleting crumbs, the gap between the economic elite and majority poor widens.[27] To divert their constituents' attention from the real issue of extreme economic disparity and gross unaccountability of elected officials, politicians routinely focus on the increasing crime rate. With the public's concern focused on crime and violence in a society that historically associates crime with Blacks, "gangsta" rap becomes an all-too-easy target. But what role do "gangsta" rap lyrics actually play in inciting and encouraging individual acts of violence?

The content of sex-violence lyrics, gun glorification, and pornographic illustrations in marketing and advertising, alleged criminal activities of some rap artists, as well as incidents in which individuals claimed rap caused them to commit crimes all contribute to this onslaught. While all music reflects and influences social reality, a cursory glace of the 1940s-1960s alone demonstrate how Black musicians interpreted, reflected, and positively inspired Black life.[28] Many of these artists were responding to the political climate and the social movements of their day. To what extent are sex-violence rap lyrics responding to the political and economic reality? Not many would agree that any significant social movement is currently functioning inside Black America. However, who can deny the Black intellectual awakening that has escalated as a result of the 1960s Black Power Movement in addition to the Black publishing efforts, independent Black schools, and general grassroots Black consciousness efforts that followed? This effort is complemented by the continuing development of an African-centered analysis for interpreting and understanding Black world reality, strengthened by the Black Studies Movement (Also referred to as Afrocentric and/or African-centered Studies). On the contemporary scene, across disciplines, John Henrik Clarke, Maulana Karenga, Haki Madhubuti, Jacob Carruthers, Frances Cress Welsing, Nathan and Julia Hare, Acklyn Lynch, Ivan Van Sertima, Marimba Ani, Molefi Asante, Sonia Sanchez, Ayi Kwei Armah, Vivian Gordon, and many others have been instrumental in documenting and shaping thought central to this worldview.

In many cases, recurring charges of "reverse racism" are a response to this awakening Black consciousness (as most whites grown accustomed to Blacks' acceptance of whites' visions of Black reality are dumbfounded by increasing Black community insistence for self-determination, self-definition and the call to re-evaluate white economic elite control of Black life). This consciousness is evident in the recent Black community support for Louis Farrakhan, Leonard Jeffries, and the unrelenting demand for Black Studies at the elementary and secondary levels. Black folks are increasingly supporting the idea that it is within our rights to defend our identification as Blacks, not apologetically as victims, but as a self-respecting and affirmatively empowered people. While some rappers are responding to and influencing these ideals, to what extent does sex-violence rap participate in this awakening?

CALL & RESPONSE AND RAP MUSIC

The call-and-response phenomenon present in various aspects of Black culture (particularly the music) best illustrates the extent to which "gangsta" rap reflects and influences current social conditions. From what community/audience are sex-violence lyrics reaffirmed? At its origin, rap music —in terms of style, lyrical content, and hardcore sound—received its affirmation from grassroots Black folk at parties, D.J. battles, etc. The commercialization of rap music, motivated by profit, effectively expanded the audience beyond Blacks to include white suburban teens, as well as the corporate recording industry's vision of rap music. The happy medium where these audiences converge is within the violent, misogynist, sexist, patriarchal attitudes that are popularly called "gangsta" rap. bell hooks writes:

> gangsta rap does not appear in a cultural vacuum but, rather, is expressive of the cultural crossing, mixing and engagement of black youth culture with the values, attitudes and concerns of the white majority....The sexist, misogynist, patriarchal ways of thinking and believing that are glorified in gangsta rap are a reflection of the prevailing values created and sustained by white supremacist capitalist patriarchy. [29]

One does not have to look far for these trends in white ruling elite America. The U.S. Navy and Senate have yet to demonstrate any serious attempt to address the misconduct of over 150 accused individuals, including officers, for their participation in what has come to be known as the 1991 Tailhook Scandal. Yale Medical School's faculty is an "old boy's network" whose sexual harassment of Ann Diamond, Joy Hersch and untold others has yet to be resolved. To date, Robert Packwood maintains his status as a U.S. Senator despite his extensive harassment of women employees (which he rationalizes by pointing out that most of the incidents happened years ago when such actions were consistent with the time). In the U.S.—when race, class, sex, and/or sexual orientation are a factor—an open eye on the double-standard reality can quickly become flooded with the neverending contradictions. The 1994 Congressional hearings on "the effects of violent and demeaning music lyrics on our nation's youth" focused on "gangsta" rap. Again, the victims of American racial violence shoulder the blame. When will the U.S. Senate hold hearings on the violence and misogyny practiced, not just spoken of, by the ruling elite?

In a highly technological, capital-driven society, where thought control via mass media permeates the society, individual worth is glorified beyond the collective, and corporate profit supersedes community interest, most rap artists are not responding to and reflecting the Black community alone. Elite visions/distortions of Black social reality are also apparent within this expression. Lacking viable alternatives, what teen-aged rapper nurtured on American values would turn down the possibility of "living large," getting "paid in full," fulfilling the American Dream of making more money in a year than most people do in a life time—knowing that both sex and violence are good for sales? Clearly, journalist David Samuels[30] and others who would blame rap for corrupting "traditional" values are misleading in their analyses. European-American capitalist values have corrupted rap music.

Despite the countless editorials, articles, and essays that flood the media suggesting the contrary, the mere presence of rap music does not explain the escalation of teen homicide. Teen homicide is on the rise across race, class, and gender, in suburban, rural, and center city communities. Gun homicide has been the leading cause of death for Black teens since 1969.[31] The expression of violent, sexist, and misogynist lyrics and the glorification of violence that persists on some rap albums and music videos, in movies, and on the streets (urban, suburban, and rural) did not begin and will not end with Black youth or rap music. ("Gangsta" rap did not even emerge until the late 1980s.) "Gangsta" rap is just one manifestation of the culture of violence that saturates American society as a whole.

As an oppressed racial group, Blacks live daily under this violence. Rap music was not necessary to motivate Colin Ferguson to violence on a Long Island train in December 1993. Daily life under the stress and strain of white supremacy and its supporting institutions was enough. On the other hand, did listening to NWA prime Jeffrey Dahmer for diabolical action? Did Michael Griffin (the gunman convicted of shooting Dr. David Gunn to death outside of the Pensacola, Florida Women's Medical Services clinic) listen to Dr. Dre's *The Chronic* in March 1993? Were the following "gangsta" rap music enthusiasts: 19-year-old James Buquet (a San Diego white male who fatally shot 4 people and then himself in October 1993), 19-year-old James Wanger (a Paterson, New Jersey white male who strangled a 17-year-old in November 1993 because he was considered a pest and a tattletale), 29-year-old Kevin Newman (a Sheridan, Wyoming white male who shot 4 children on a school yard and then shot himself in

September 1993), 34-year-old Joel Rifkin (a white male who confessed to killing 18 women in the New York City metropolitan area in September 1993), 62-year-old Gordon Neumann (a white male who shot to death a woman and a child and wounded 5 others before shooting himself to death in November 1993), and 39-year-old Danny Rolling (a white male who confessed to the 1990 mutilation murders of 5 University of Florida students in Gainsville)? Did these violent individuals explore "gangsta" rap music for their values? These horror stories suggest that there are very specific conditions in American society that nurture violent individual expression, and "gangsta" rap is a by-product of, not a prerequisite for, that violence.

GUN VIOLENCE AND RAP MUSIC

Amidst the sexism, misogyny, and stereotypical portrayals of Blacks, rap artists glorify gun violence primarily in three contexts: (1) as a symbol of macho power, (2) as a cure-all for disputes between Blacks, and (3) as a necessity for individual protection. These fantasies prevail from album covers and advertisements to rap videos, magazines, newspaper interviews and articles. The November 1992 issue of *The*

Source highlighted on its cover a photo of Dr. Dre holding an automatic handgun to his head. Similarly, *Seconds* magazine highlighted on the cover the rap group House of Pain, with one of the rappers holding a handgun in the air. Both Ice T's *Iceberg* and Eazy E's *Wanted* album covers prominently exhibit guns. Although KRS-ONE was one of the first rappers to display guns on his album cover (*Criminal Minded*), he explained that his intentions were not to pose as a gangster, but to encourage Blacks to "stop the violence" against each other and to stop being the victims of white-on-Black violence (in its various forms) "by all means necessary."[32] However, once this concept was actualized as a sales pitch, countless rappers began to catalog guns in their lyrics as well as in marketing their albums. This trend has become particularly disturbing within rap music videos, where often rappers act out narrations of Black-on-Black violence. Both the lyrics and the video images bring attention to various automatic weapons—Uzis, Tec-9s, Glock 9 mms, etc.

Given the extensive influence that rap artists maintain among Black youth, perception of the use of guns are widely affected by these images. The tremendous amount of individual insecurity that persists among many Black youth is articulated in some rap artists' justification of their need for weapons. The proliferation of guns in urban communities only serves to heighten such insecurities.

The issue of guns and violence amongst Black youth is quite complex. The sense of hopelessness and despair that currently manifests itself in a so-called gangster mentality demands more careful and in-depth study. While the existence of an underground economy in Black urban America is not new, the availability of guns, the level of self-hatred, the quantity and potency of drugs, the unique insecurities, and the extreme Black youth poverty all create a self-destructive situation unparalleled in Black American history. Black youth are further vulnerable for various reasons: family difficulties, individual ability and life circumstances, position of relative Black powerlessness as well as the anti-Black manner in which Blacks are interpreted and defined in American society. The crisis situation escalates as these insecurities are coupled with the glorification and availability of guns. Most often, youth feel a need to have guns for protection against the threat of others having them (again, insecurity). Rather than waiting to become victims, many are going on the offensive. However, Black youth do not control the illegal gun trade and the easy access that youth have to guns cannot be attributed to rap music.

Although such gun glorification does not begin or end in the Black community, rap music may be the first arena in American society where Blacks have romanticized gun violence—not as a solution for our problems with ruling elite America, but as solutions for our disputes between one another. Black youth must be held accountable for their actions, but simply condemning and reprimanding them is not enough. Part of the solution lies in Black youth becoming more responsible for Black survival and development. The conditions that allow the easy access of illegal guns must be disrupted.

Many conservative, liberal, and misinformed whites and Blacks resent references to Black homicide in its many guises as a conspiracy. Yet, until federal, state, and local governments demonstrate a serious commitment to ending illegal gun and drug entry into Black communities, who can deny the parallels between the current reality and the planned genocide of Native Americans via guns, drugs (alcohol), and other forces?

America's gun glorification has an extensive history. Let us not overlook President Bill Clinton's recollection as he signed the Brady bill into law:

I can still remember the first day when I was a

> little boy out in the country putting the can on
> top of a fence post and shooting a .22 at it...This
> is part of the culture of a big part of America.

This is not merely a nostalgic recollection. President Clinton knows that his experience is not unlike many Americans with whom he identifies. Hollywood understands this also and has been instrumental in advancing gun symbolism and images of violence in cartoons, "family" television programs, and R-rated movies. Sex-violence rap music is not the first to use sex and gun imagery to increase sales. This glorification is intensified by the constant threat of violence posed by local, state, and federal law enforcement agencies. In general, these agencies do not protect people. Their role is to maintain the status quo, and their "kick-ass" image and history reinforce America's culture of violence. While these agencies play "cowboy" for the economic elite, who will protect the children and make it possible for them to grow up without fear of being violated?

As long as children do not feel secure in their own communities, neighborhoods, homes, and schools, as long as the capitalist ethic of individualism as well as extreme poverty and unemployment persists, youth will carry and use weapons. In many cases, guns will be used as a means of self-defense. In other situations, automatic weapons will be used in Black-on-Black criminal and violent activity. This reality is not an excuse for rap artists to glorify guns, primarily as weapons to be used against people of color. Although "gangsta" rap is not responsible for violence in America, in glorifying Black-on-Black violence sex-violence rap lyrics contribute to a climate that suggests that such violence is acceptable. Given the extensive level to which "gangsta" rap saturates Black youth environments, and given the very negative, self-hating, and anti-Black worldview that sex-violence lyrics condone, youth perceptions of the role of violence are distorted.

The highly publicized incidents of gun violence involving rap artists are important because they reveal the artists' individual insecurities despite their financial success and fame as rappers. The media coverage of these incidents is one-sided, sensationalized, without in-depth analysis and perpetuates the image of Blacks as violence-prone. Depictions of this type encourages the general public to believe that rap music and Black youth are responsible for gun violence in America.

Without question, the social/political vision of rap artists who advocate sex-violence themes needs expansion. That such rappers have achieved the proverbial "American Dream" underscores the fact that the problems Blacks face go beyond poverty. The dominant image of guns within the context of rap music is ultimately self-hating, places power in the gun, and further disempowers the collective Black community. Many young rap artists do not perceive the damage they do with these individualist acts, which suggests how thoroughly America's cult of individualism pervades Black America. Realistic and attainable (short- and long-term) alternatives must be explored to correct these compounded problems.

A VICTIM'S WORLDVIEW: GANGSTERS, PLAYERS, PIMPS, HUSTLERS...

As so-called gangsta rap began to make its mark as more than a short-lived part of the rap music continuum, Black community concern about its effects began to escalate. This concern is expressed in protest demonstrations, radio station policy decisions, and in community discussions. In a 1992 Chicago community forum, Maulana Karenga stated,

> Rap had a glorious beginning....it put a Black sound out again...it restored the creativity and distinctiveness of Black music...it reaffirmed community as a fundamental factor of music.[33]

Rap music's transformation from that glorious beginning to a place where sex-violence lyrics occupy its center indicates the destructive effects of Black America's limited community control, particularly in the very sacred arena of culture. The corruption and commodification of rap music serves as a blueprint for the economic elite and as yet another warning for Black America. If Black people did not send our youth outside of our community to acquire values, culture, and vision, then our political empowerment and Black youth understanding their responsibility to the Black community would not be left up to chance.

In terms of Black sound, creativity and distinctiveness, many "gangsta" rappers, as a result of our collective increasing political consciousness, have resisted giving up ultimate control. (This is apparent in some rappers' efforts to establish independent record labels.) However, in the areas of community-responsiveness and participation as a fundamental factor in Black music, sex-violence rap artists prove deficient. Where is the Black cultural tradition's moral center articulated in sex-violence rap?

The often mythical world that "gangsta" rap presents as reality is a world that glorifies crime, guns, drug-selling and drug-using, sexual exploitation, irresponsible parenthood, Black-on-Black homicide, women as inferiors and objects, gang-life, 40-ounce drinking as routine, and extreme materialism. It is a world in which profanity persists for profanity's sake and the acquisition of money remains central. Snoop Doggy Dogg's chorus for "Gin and Juice" sings,

> rolling down the street smoking indo, sipping on gin and juice, with my mind on my money and my money on my mind (*Doggystyle*).

On Too Short's album, *Short Dog's in the House*, rapper Ice Cube raps,

> Now stupid little bitches get tossed / If they don't realize that I'm the mothafuckin boss / Come on down and get your ass pinched / and if you talk shit, you get your ass lynched / Cause I'm the b-i-t-c-h k-i-l-l-a /
> Ice Cube's a nigga that's bigga than a nut / Cause a bitch is a bitch is a hoe is a slut ("Nothin But a Word").

In the same rap song, Too Short suggests that a "real" man is one who is not afraid to get physical with women. A man who does not physically abuse a woman who questions his actions is defined as a "bitch" as well:

> You come home and get smooth cussed out / you got a bitch with a foul ass mouth / you're scared to serve her with a left hook / then nigga you're a bitch in my book.

The worldview of "gangsta" rappers is further characterized by the lyrics of songs like Too

Short's "Players Life," where Too Short shares his views on marriage, "I made up my mind at seventeen / no engagement for me and no wedding ring / I'll be a player for life." The valuelessness of women in this worldview is reflected in such statements as "women come a dime a dozen," "I'll give you my girl, but I won't give you a joint," and "coming up we learn how to break these tramps / and when you through, then you shake these tramps / and when you're older its just like a routine."

For those who would argue that this is Black culture, where is the sense of African spirituality and humanity in these perspectives of male/female interaction? In this "gangsta" world women are dehumanized, hold less value than drugs, and are only worthy as sexual objects to be conquered, used, traded, and given away. Additionally, Black males learn destructive values in childhood that they maintain as adults, without questioning or rethinking their usefulness or uselessness. Whatever the moral or immoral center that exists there, it persists in Smif N' Wessun's "Bucktown," Ice Cube's "Bonnie and Clyde," Snoop Doggy Dogg's "Gz Up Hoes Down" and Luther Campbell's "Baby Dick." Likewise, Dr. Dre raps:

never let me slip cause if I slip then I'm slipping

> / but if I got my nina then you know I'm
> straight trippin / And I'ma continue to put the
> rap down, put the mac down / and if you
> bitches talk shit, I have to put the smack down.
> ("Nothing But a G-Thang").

As inanimate objects, women (as bitches, hoes, skeezers, freaks, trix) are not to have opinions. In fact, a thinking woman who questions (*i.e.* "talkin shit") incites the physical violence ("put the smack down") of her male peers.

Many rap artists and enthusiasts argue that these are simply songs about reality, but not reality itself. Yet, the psychological implications and subliminal messages define the parameters of a worldview constructed around Black inhumanity. The implications of these messages only intensify when rap artists act out their narrations. Case in point: Dr. Dre's alleged vicious beating of Dee Barnes (former hostess of now defunct *Pump It Up*), which was widely known among rap enthusiasts, but barely discussed in the larger Black community. Supposedly, Barnes moved out of her assigned role as a woman, and the artists alleged response mirrors the lyrics' suggestion.[34]

We should not deceive ourselves with the false assumption that such views are confined to the so-called underclass, "ghetto" community. Although many men publicly state that they are working to move toward more enlightened understandings of and interactions with women, who among us, regardless of socio-economic status, has not heard of or experienced incidents of blatant Black male sexism? Most certainly, the articulations of some rap artists are not isolated incidents or perspectives. A great deal of confusion and pain persists in Black male anti-woman attitudes toward Black women. The victim's worldview espoused by "gangster" rappers is not an aberration; these non-developmental perspectives permeate the Black community and American society as a whole and immediate, ongoing action must be taken to reverse these trends. Some rappers resist these images in their lyrics (*i.e.*, Queen Latifah's U.N.I.T.Y and KRS-ONE's Brown Skin Woman), but their voices remain an acute minority.

The offensive repressive attitude of women in this victim's context often overpowers the perceptions of Black men, which are equally alarming. In this worldview, Black male youth are savage, devoid of vision, non-thinking, incapable of love, violence-prone, and ultimately, schizophrenic. Possibilities for "real" Black men are limited to the pimp, the player, the drug dealer, the gangster, the mack, or the hustler. They are defined and assume the identity of losers, victims that enthusiastically achieve their role as statistics, killers, void of spiritual centers, rapists, and fighters only against Black life and possibilities. The relationships of Black male youth to their nuclear and extended family and community are confined as follows:

1) they love and respect their biological mothers via lip service;

2) they maintain a steady flow of hatred, disappointment and disrespect for biological fathers and by extensions failed Black male "role models," who either abandoned them or have given up their manhood via cooperation with "the system";

3) they have siblings that are trapped in the systemic cycles of death;

4) they lack respect for Black female peers, who are viewed as *hoes, skeezers, trix, gold diggers, bitches* and, by extension, sources of sexual satisfaction that no matter how distorted, border on hatred;

5) finally, they claim they "still got love for" their Black male peers, homeboys, homeys, "my niggaz," although the call for violence is often against Black male peers and homosexuality is an unacceptable option.

The pimp, gangster, player, mack-daddy, and hustler glorified in sex-violence rap never asks before taking action the critical question, "is it best for Black people?" These oppressive representations of Black women, men, and Black life must be resisted. This worldview leaves very little possibility for development even at the most fundamental level. Unfortunately, for too many Black youth, definitions of Black womanhood and manhood are derived from this context. With such alienated and disintegrated visions of one's self and one's people, how does one move beyond a mere survivalist mentality?

FRAGMENTS OF
BLACK POLITICAL CONSCIOUS

Beneath the extreme vulgarities and profanities of the anti-Black worldview of "gangsta" rappers, there persists in some sex-violence lyrics various levels of consciousness of the social forces that bring this victim's world into existence. Dr. Dre reveals an accurate understanding of America's racial politics when he raps,

> Why do I call myself a nigga you ask me/ cause my mouth is so mothafuckin nasty/ bitch this bitch that nigga this nigga that/ Gettin paid to say this shit here/ makin more in a month than a doctor makes in a year/ So why not call myself a nigga/ It's better than pulling a trigger and going up the river/ And then I get called a nigga anyway/ broke as mothafucka and locked away/ So to cut out all that bullshit / I guess I'll be a nigga for life" ("Niggaz 4 Life").

The inhumanities of capitalism and the failure of Black politicians who regularly compromise in their search for Black political empowerment is evident when Ice Cube raps, do I have to sell me a whole lot of crack / for decent shelter and clothes on my back? / Or should I just wait for help from Bush / or Jesse Jackson and Operation Push ("A Bird in the Hand").

Placing their hopes on a tomorrow that never arrives, many Black politicians become enmeshed in activities that never significantly transform the reality of the Black poor. For many poor Blacks, the major alternative for survival too often remains the underground economy. Snoop Doggy Dogg raps,

we expose ways for the youth to survive / Some think its wrong but we tend to think its right / So make all them ends you can make / cause when you're broke you break ("Little Ghetto Boys").

The reality that these lyrics address can not be denied. These representations identify *some* options for Blacks as well as a *part* of Black life in America.

Guns, gangs, violence, death, hunger, and dis-ease are phenomena common to oppressed, impoverished environments. Various sex-violence rap lyrics accurately present *some* aspects of urban street life, but to glorify this poverty/ street life culture and embrace it as the norm for Black life is misleading. This view of Black poverty is one-dimensional and stereotypical. Just as it is reductive to think of the Black community as a monolithic one, it is destructive to accept distorted visions of Black culture. Blacks involved in these gang-type, hustler lifestyles are the exception rather than the rule. Additionally, the assumption that street culture is rebellious in general, and against the status quo, specifically, is false. Those Blacks who advocate street culture reinforce the white economic elite's agenda for Blacks, demonstrating the depth of Black economic and political powerlessness. Street culture encourages neither independence nor development, but further victimization of Black youth through Black-on-Black crime, prison, drug addiction, and death. There is nothing about street culture that is rebellious, revolutionary, or pro-Black. Most sex-violence lyrics do not offer solutions at all, but see Black oppression as an end in itself. The solution, it seems, is extreme individualism. (As several rap artists rap, "You gotta get yours, I gotta get mine.") Most poor Blacks are hardworking and struggling to make it day-to-day, while lacking any significant range of job opportunities or independent cultural institutions needed to influence change.

Further, Black Americans as a people, regardless of their socio-economic status, are not respected by the collective white economic elite. (If one doubts this, consider the implications of the U.S. failure to recognize Black America's call for reparations for the inhumane crimes committed against African Americans during the American slavery experience.) As Blackness and Black culture is degraded, Blacks are subject to harassment, violation, and unjust imprisonment—just because we are Black! Some sex-violence rappers accurately assess the destructive impacts of a minimum wage and/or jobless existence, whose only other options are the military or the underground economy. This reality is not simply a Black one, but demonstrates at a day-to-day level the pitfalls of capitalism and white racism as they impact Black life. Still, this victim's reality is not one to glorify. To accept and participate in this reality as an end in and of itself suggests acceptance of defeat. Here rap artists play out white supremacist dreams of the inferior Black, but where is the Black vision?

RECOMMENDATIONS

As far as influence in the Black community, no group has as extensive an influence as rap artists in terms of their ability to capture the listening ear of Black youth—not the Black athlete, not the Black entertainer, not the politician, the teacher, nor the Christian or Muslim minister. Notice the extensive influence that some rappers have demonstrated in moving Black youth toward more natural hairstyles (i.e., afros and braids). Black Nationalist efforts have been consistent in attempts to raise the level of Black consciousness in many areas, including hair. These efforts are certainly apparent in general increasing Black community consciousness, but few of these efforts have permeated youth culture as directly as rap has. Our individual and collective ability to move forward, to mature politically and culturally, will determine what will be made of this influence.

Across the board, the real challenge remains to similarly encourage the death of age-old women-hating and anti-Black visions via sex-violence lyrics. Rap artists must understand that all culture is political. Because American democracy, despite its rhetoric has historically blocked Blacks from developing life-sustaining options, individual success does not translate into change for the collective. Thus, a rapper's individual "making it" should not be at the expense of the collective community. Each individual must strike a balance between that which is in his/her best interest as well as the overall community. Too often, individualism has compromised Black collective advancement.

Rap artists can have a voice that is not ultimately demeaning to themselves and their communities despite the extensive impact of corporate elite structures. The independent Black books movement in this country demonstrates how Blacks can creatively impact an industry without imitating it. In the final analysis, hardcore rap artists' control of the evolving definitions of rap music will be determined by (1) their willingness to seize control of production and distribution and (2) their ability to strategically control their participation in various forms of mass media.

Currently, America's white nationalist[35] (mainstream) institutions are producing neither solutions to the problems facing Black America nor developmental alternatives for Black life in any area. The music industry is no different. The "gangsta" rap group NWA emerged in the late 1980s alongside the more politically conscious Public Enemy. By that time, Boogie Down Productions, had already distinguished itself as a conscious and hardcore rap group. Where would Black youth be headed today had public interest centered around conscious rap rather than sex-violence rap? As long as rap artists depend exclusively on the corporate-controlled, market-driven recording industry and economic elite-influenced mass media, their definitions and images will be distorted. The commercialization of rap music has broadened rap's economic base, but simultaneously constricted the voice of the rapper's themselves and the community from which they emerge. Enlightened independent development remains critical.[36]

Critics of "gangsta" rappers must not become apologists for the street culture mentality that permeates "gangsta" rap lyrics. Yet, they must keep in mind that most of these rap artists are under twenty-five years old. Although they have already made a considerable impact as artists, they still have many years ahead of them to grow and develop politically and creatively. The rapper Ice Cube, for example, gained national recognition with NWA in the late 1980s. Today, Ice Cube's lyric content has expanded beyond their sex-violence origins. We all want others to provide for the possibility of change in ourselves, but few people allow that space for others. Often, when the critic comes in peace, love, and sincerity, he/she is more likely to earn a sympathetic ear.

Kalamu ya Salaam argues that Africans in America are a unique people, are blues people. Just as we evolved the original blues musical artform, that "blues aesthetic" is the essence we must reclaim in order to remain centered in ourselves:

> Recognized or not, blues people manifest a blues sensibility. After two or three generations, that manifestation is culturally codified into an aesthetic which shows out in everything done, not just in the music...the end of African American mass espousal of the blues aesthetic is marked by the wholesale acceptance of integration and the concurrent destruction of our working class economy...Once a decision was made by the masses to try integrating into the American cultural mainstream, the blues aesthetic ceased to be the dominant mode of cultural expression precisely because it was not only not like the mainstream, it was often anti mainstream, clashing in values and indices of beauty."[37]

Rap music at the grassroots/hardcore level reflects this concept of the blues aesthetic. The challenge to rap artists is to stay on the mark, study Black culture, and thus keep the tradition alive.

Gil Scott-Heron is a fine example of this study-oriented, teaching musician. He has given us a great deal of inspirational and rejuvenating music across three decades. His latest release, *Spirits* (TVT Records, 1994), contains the song, "Message to the Messengers," which is directed specifically to rap artists:

> I ain't comin at you with no disrespect/ All I'm saying is that you damn well got to be correct/ Cause if you gonna be speaking for a whole generation/ And you know enough to handle

their education/ be sure you know the real deal about past situations...

things don't go both ways/ You can't talk respect on every other song or every other day/...Four letter words don't make you a poet/ they'll just magnify how shallow you are and let everybody know it....

His words are insightful, poetic, instructive, and, as always, prophetic. Gil Scott-Heron's work, in addition to the history of rap and Black music, needs to be studied. The best music that Blacks have produced has always asked us to reach deep inside ourselves for the best in us.

As one who has maintained a steady presence and consistent voice within rap music, KRS-ONE puts forth a similar effort. He continues to expand his creativity with each album. Keeping his eye and ear on Black history and struggle, he remains tuned into the pulse of our present reality. Other rap artists should listen to him more closely and follow his example. We do not need to produce clones. Each artist must define his/her own creative voice while remaining true to the artform, the Black community, and to himself/herself. Such an approach could parallel the beginnings of many of the Black Fire poets, who were community-centered and study-oriented. While independently innovative, they recognized the value of learning from community elders and historians how to develop into responsible Black cultural workers. They remained committed to people first and understood that as people of African descent, it is part of our cultural imperative to "leave our communities more beautiful then we found them."[38] This is the real challenge of rap music: to actualize and heighten raps potential as an agent of social change rather than being enslaved by "mainstream," commercial popular culture. In all areas of human interaction, Blacks must resist being misused by others. And as we continue to transform our reality, we cannot allow narrow-mindedness, naivete, or deceitful manipulation from within or outside of our community to control that destiny.

Rap artists, rap enthusiasts, and general listeners must go beyond hardcore, *phat* beats and approach substance. We need positive, progressive, liberating action in our communities. Political consciousness needs to be raised. We need rap music that not only stays true to hardcore, underground funk (*i.e.*, blues aesthetic), but further encourages study, struggle, dialogue, activism, creativity, discipline, community-centeredness, healing, and respect for Black life. We need rap music that stays true, but simultaneously expands the discourse beyond the limited imagination of individual egos, materialism, and distorted (deforming) sexual desires. We need economic and political enlightened empowerment, and rap artists too must continue to contribute to that effort through enlightened and creative lyrics and style, creating and supporting independent Black institutions, continuing to provide space to explore youth concerns, supporting national and international human rights efforts, advancing enlightened perspectives of women and respect for Black life, creating jobs to assist communities in need, and exploring alternatives for those of us whose days are filled with more hopelessness than happiness.

Disrupting the regressive trends that have come to be acceptable by many most certainly will not be an overnight process. It will require hard work and continuous effort to negotiate the multiple terrains which allow sex-violence attitudes, corporate exploitation, and economic elitism to persist. The rewards for these efforts are many, but first we must regain the confidence that despite the seemingly invincible status quo, as a collective committed to change, we have the power to construct a better world. Each of us has a circle of influence within which we must constantly challenge, re-examine, and disrupt outdated patterns of thinking and interacting. Through our efforts, our dreams of equality, mutual respect, and empowerment can and will be reality.

What role will rap music play in this struggle? Novelist Paule Marshall writes, "the woods are on fire out here...and we need everybody who can tote a bucket of water to come running."[39] Rap music stands at the crossroads, as we all do. Will we participate in and escalate our own oppression, or will we dare to rise above our shortcomings and struggle daily for the best in us?

Notes

1. "Enlightened empowerment" is a term used by Haki Madhubuti. See his *Claiming Earth: Race, Rage, Rape, Redemption; Blacks Seeking A Culture of Enlightened Empowerment* (Chicago: Third World Press), 1994. It is an important distinction, "enlightened" as opposed to simply "empowerment." Madhubuti insists that as we search for empowerment, Blacks must not seek to duplicate much of the saneness that passes as normal by the minority elite who currently holds economic and political power at the expense of the majority and most certainly the planet. Throughout this essay, I refer to the minority elite as "the economic elite."

2. "So-called" because the activity attributed to gangsters are not isolated to *the street*, but permeates the society. The actions of the some American institutions, such as the CIA and FBI, as well as individuals like junk-bond trader Michael Milken and even former president George Bush, to name a few, exhibit gangster-like tendencies. Yet they are never referred to as gangsters. Therefore, to refer to Black rappers this way is misleading and stereotypical. Further, the term "gangster rap" is very vague, and does not explain the extent to which sex and violence imagery permeates rap music.

3. Michael Dyson, "Bum Rap," the *New York Times*, (February 3, 1994), p. A13.

4. "Rap Band Members Found Not Guilty In Obscenity Trial," the *New York Times* (October 19, 1990).

5. For background information on rap music, see James Spady's and Joseph Eure's *Nation Conscious Rap* (Brooklyn: PC International Press), 1991; Michael Small's *Break it Down: The Inside Story from the New Leaders of Rap* (New Jersey:

Citadel Press), 1992; Nelson Havelock's and Michael Gonzales' *Bring the Noise: A Guide to Rap Music and Hip Hop Culture* (New York: Harmony Books), 1991; and Tricia Rose's *Black Noise: Rap Music and Black Culture in Contemporary America* (Hanover, NH: Wesleyan University), 1994.

6. KRS-ONE (Kris Parker) "The Original Way," *Sex and Violence*, Jive/RCA, 1992.

7. By "commercialization" I mean economic elite corporate involvement in rap music with profit as its chief aim. Commercialization means to exploit mainly for financial gain, sacrificing the quality for profit. The use of the term commercialization is not meant to suggest that because an artist's material is selling he or she is a commercial artist. The term "commercialized rap" in this essay refers to the work of rap artists whose styles have been altered or constructed around being rewarded financially—not for being true to themselves, the artform or rap origins, but to the white corporate elite interest (that which is in the best interest of increasing sales rather than elevating the artform). Some hardcore rappers do achieve commercial success with some records. This does not mean that they have crossed over, or have become commercialized artists, but that they have been able to capitalize on consumer taste and that there is a demand for the type of music (hardcore rap) that they produce.

8. Amy Linden, "The Grand Old Men Strike Back," the *New York Times*, p. H33.

9. See Jerry Mander's *In the Absence of the Sacred*, (San Francisco: Sierra Club Books), 1991, p. 129.

10. David Samuels, "The Rap on Rap: The Black Music That Isn't Either," *New Republic*, Vol. 205 (November 11, 1991), p. 24-25. Although Samuels' essay carefully documents some important facts about rap, sometimes taken out of context, it is most

problematic because the author places Blacks—
rap artists and listeners—on the periphery of rap
music and whites at the center, insisting that
white men were ultimately responsible for the
emergence and development of rap music and
not merely for its commercialization. In *Black
Noise: Rap Music and Black Culture in Contemporary America*, Tricia Rose suggests that Black buying and listening patterns are undermined by the
SoundScan computer system for tracking sales.

11. SoundScan (Interview), May 13, 1994.
12. This tendency was given insightful treatment in
    the satirical film *CB4*, which focuses on a rap
    "artist" who co-opts a criminal's image.
13. *Nation Conscious Rap*, p.5.
14. See Marimba Ani's *Let the Circle Be Unbroken*
    (Trenton: Red Sea Press), 1992. Also Kalamu ya
    Salaam's "the blues aesthetic" in *What is Life:
    Reclaiming the Black Blues Self* (Chicago: Third
    World Press), 1994.
15. For general background information, see *The Directory of Corporate Affiliations* (New York: Reed
    Publishing), 1994.
16. Ibid.
17. Bandar Artist Management, Central Islip, NY
    (Interview). Several other independent management companies provided critical interviews
    which helped me to document this trend. For the
    sake of confidentiality, I leave their names off the
    record. Also, see "Relativity's Rap Family is
    Growing: Market Deals up Label Street Profile."
    Billboard Magazine (February 26, 1994), p. 13.
18. Hashim Shomari, *From the Underground: Hip Hop
    as an Agent for Social Change* (unpublished manuscript). Shomari has argued for years that hip-hop culture is an anti-establishment culture and
    therefore rap music can play a positive role in
    radical Black struggle by providing alternative

sources of information (like the drum for enslaved Africans in America during American slavery). Whereas the drum was banned by the
slaveholders, the contemporary economic elite
have grown more sophisticated in their response
to Black resistance to cultural, political, and economic imperialism. Today the economic elite
counters such resistance by simply co-opting the
resistance effort.

19. "Fresh Air," National Public Radio (May 16, 1994).
20. Haki Madhubuti, "Language: Is There a Black
    Way?" *Claiming Earth: Race, Rage, Rape, Redemp-
    tion; Blacks Seeking a Culture of Enlightened Empow-
    erment* (Chicago: Third World Press), 1994.
21. Houston Baker carefully critiques this trend in
    his *Black Studies, Rap and the Academy* (Chicago:
    University of Chicago Press), 1993. He describes
    it as "a totally self-interested form of popular
    hucksterism" (p.81). Baker offers an informed
    reflection on the Black academic's responsibility
    to rap music rather than trivializing or mystify-
    ing rap. Michael Dyson's essays, "The Culture of
    Hip Hop," and "Rap Music and Black Culture,"
    in *Reflecting Black* (Minneapolis: Univ. Minnesota
    Press), 1993 and Greg Tate's essay "Above and
    Beyond Rap's Decibels," the *New York Times*
    (March 6, 1994), Section 2, p. 1&36 demonstrate
    analyses of rap without criticism of the roles of
    corporate elitism or racism in instigating various
    shortcomings. While I disagree with their no-
    tions of Black culture becoming universal and rap
    music as "a staple in American culture," both
    writers make several insightful points about rap
    music.
22. Sheila Rule, "Generation Rap," the *New York
    Times* (April 3, 1994), pp. 42-45.
23. Lecture at African American Book Center, Chi-
    cago, IL (March 27, 1992). Also see handout,

"Understanding Rap's Mixed Messages," from Seminar in Social Theory and Practice XIV, Institute of Pan African Studies (Summer 1991) and his revised and expanded edition of *Introduction to Black Studies* (Los Angeles: University of Sankore Press), 1993.

24. The term "Conscious Rap" builds upon the concept of "Nation Conscious Rap," elevated in *Nation Conscious Rap*, by James Spady and Joseph Eure. (Brooklyn: PC International Press), 1991.

25. This is not to suggest that the blues are sexist-free. However, blues music does not approach the obscenities and vulgarities that characterize "gangsta" rap.

26. Lecture at African American Book Center, Chicago, IL. (March 1992).

27. See my "Violence, Doublespeak, and the American Ruling Elite," *Why LA Happened: Implications of the 1992 Los Angeles Rebellion* (Chicago: Third World Press), 1993. Also see Noam Chomsky's *The Prosperous Few and Restless Many* (Berkeley: Odonian Press), 1993.

28. Acklyn Lynch, *Nightmare Overhanging Darkly: Essays on Black Culture and Resistance*. (Chicago: Third World Press), 1992. Also in his presentation in a forum on Black Cultural Resistance at the African American Book Center Chicago, IL (February 19, 1994) he discussed the political insights of some "gangsta" rappers.

29. bell hooks, "Sexism and Misogyny: Who Takes the Rap?; Misogyny, Gangsta Rap and the Piano," *Z Magazine*, February 1994, p. 26.

30. "The Rap on Rap: The 'Black Music' That Isn't Either," *New Republic*, (November 11, 1991), pp. 24-25.

31. Lois Fingerhut, Deborah Ingram, and Jacob Feldman. "Firearm Homicide Among Black Teenage Males in Metropolitan Counties," *Journal of*

the American Medical Association. Vol 267, No. 22. (June 10, 1992), p. 3054.

32. Kris Parker (KRS-ONE), *By All Means Necessary,* Jive/RCA, 1989.

33. Maulana Karenga Lecture at African American Book Center, Chicago, IL. (March 1992).

34. Although Dr. Dre. denies beating Dee Barnes, this is her account of what happened: " Dr. Dre picks me up by my shirt in the front and I can't even say 'help' cause I'm choking....Then, Dre picks me up by my hair and ear and starts slamming my face up against...a brick wall." See "Sista Dee Speaks," Louis Flores, *The Source* (December 1992). Also, "Moving Target," *The Source*, (November 1992). See also Pearl Cleage, "Down Wit Dee," *Deals with the Devil and Other Reasons to Riot* (New York: Ballantine) 1993. Barnes subsequently sued Dr. Dre. Hours before jury selection began, Dr. Dre and Dee Barnes settled out of court for an undisclosed six-figure dollar amount. *Dallas Morning News* (October 3, 1993).

35. My use of the term white nationalist is not meant to suggest Black nationalism in white face. White American nationalism is concerned with self-preservation and elevation of the white race as well as oppression of other races. White nationalism views oppression of other racial groups as fundamental to white development. This concept is carefully explained in the work of John Henrik Clarke (*Notes For An African World Revolution: African People at the Crossroads*), Frances Cress Welsing (*The Isis Papers: The Keys to the Colors*), Bobby Wright (*The Psychopathic Racial Personality*), Marimba Ani (*Yurugu: An African-centered Critique of European Cultural Thought and Behavior*), Haki Madhubuti (*Enemies: The Clash of Races*), and others. Most major European-Centered American Institutions, including public schools,

state and federal governments, corporate industry, etc., reflect this ideology. I am speaking here in terms of whites as a collective, not strictly as individuals. Enlightened Black Nationalism, while concerned with Black world preservation and development, does not see the hatred, oppression, and/or domination of other racial groups as fundamental to Black survival. From this perspective, operating out of an understanding of African spirituality and humanism, peaceful co-existence is desired. As Black people continue to be exploited and degraded, this philosophical and ideological worldview embraces and elevates Black life. This is not reverse racism. The goal is not to trumpet Blackness as superior or to imply that others are inferior. The emphasis is on self-development, self-respect, self-defense, and self-determination.

36. For example, Dr. Dre's Death Row, Eazy E's Ruthless Records, Luther Campbell's Luke Records. Just as these examples suggest, without consciousness and vision, Black independent efforts may not reach their potential. However, Shomari (*From the Underground*) insists that if these artist develop a worldview that moves them beyond confines of status quo possibilities, they will have an established base from which to begin development.

37. Kalamu ya Salaam, "the blues aesthetic," *What is Life?: Reclaiming the Black Blues Self* (Chicago: Third World Press), 1994.

38. Karenga, *The African American Holiday of Kwanzaa* (Los Angeles: University of Sankore Press), 1988.

39. Paule Marshall, *Daughters* (New York: Antheneum), 1991, p. 102.

About the Author

Bakari Kitwana is currently Executive Editor and Assistant to the Publisher at Third World Press. He is also Managing Editor of *Black Books Bulletin: Words Work*. His essay "Violence, Doublespeak and the American Ruling Elite" appeared in the anthology *Why LA Happened: Implications of the 1992 Los Angeles Rebellion*. He has also contributed to the collection *Confusion By Any Other Name*. Kitwana holds Masters degrees in English and Education from the University of Rochester and is currently completing a book-length study on Black teen gun homicide.